UNMASKED

Breaking Generational Curses and
Experiencing Authentic Purpose

BRYAN D. EVANS, SR.

Title: Unmasked
Subtitle: Breaking Generational Curses & Experiencing Authentic Purpose
ISBN: 978-1-952327-49-0
Library of Congress Control Number: 2021903082

Definitions referenced from *Merriam-Webster.com*. 2021. https://www.merriam-webster.com

This book is creative fiction in the form of a memoir. It reflects the author's recollections of experiences over time. Some names and characteristics have been changed, some events have been compressed, and some dialogue has been recreated. Any resemblance to actual persons, living or dead, or actual events is purely coincidental. The publisher and author are not responsible for any offense, injury, or liability claimed by the reader.

T.A.L.K. Publishing
5215 North Ironwood Road, Suite 200
Glendale, WI 53217
publishwithtalk.com

talkconsulting.net

UNMASKED

ACKNOWLEDGEMENTS

First, I devote this book to Algie, David, and Joyce, for their lives and struggles were the inspiration for this story and the catalyst for the man I am today.

Second, to Darla, my mother, your sacrifices, despite all the obstacles you faced in your life, don't go unnoticed. I desire that God grant you the strength to fight until you have fulfilled His purpose for your life.

Third, to the man who provided the physical seed that gave me life, here's to you. In the pages of this book, I find the strength to forgive you and believe that my life's events were necessary for me to be who God ordained me to be. Your absence, while painful, was required, so oddly enough, I thank you.

Finally, but certainly not least, I devote the pages of this book to my wife, affectionately known as Gigi, and my children, Bryan Jr., and Gabrielle, who have always loved me for me, flaws and all. To them, I pledge to live up to the man you all need me to be, unmasked, free of generational curses, living freely, in purpose, authentically.

INTRODUCTION

The year is 2020, and everyone is wearing a mask. Publicly, people show that they are doing their part to protect themselves and others from a virus that threatens to alter our very civilization. These masks seem to have only replaced the unseen metaphorical masks we have always worn—masks that obscure who we are, dispensed by people who endeavor to ensure that people of color never procure a life of liberty, peace, or pleasure.

Undoubtedly, we can agree that we have all worn masks. We placed on these masks to protect us from the painful intentions of those who mean to destroy us. Some of us wear masks to hide hateful feelings of unsubstantiated disgust, hiding the promotion of unjust deeds. White hoods, gold shields, black robes, and flag pins symbolically mask hatred toward people of color. These metaphorical masks, replaced by literal ones, now allow us to finally see the real chaos in our communities, unveiling what has always been—disunity.

Divided by race, religion, and party, the physical masks have emboldened us to spew out hatred with no regard, conspicuously. Unfortunately, in some respect, each of us has metaphorically masked areas of our lives, often unaware that the mask is a part of the construct of our reality. Now that covering our faces has become a trendsetting fashion statement, it seems as if we have let our guard down, becoming comfortable, for better or for worse, with displaying our true inner selves. Not everyone who wears a mask is hiding hatred and evil toward others blatantly. Some of us use our disguise to hide internal struggles and the emotions that hinder us from being our authentic selves.

This story guides the reader through historical accounts of my life and lineage in hopes that readers will identify with one or more of the characters. Each character has their own story of hidden emotions that develop internal struggles. These struggles continue to propagate from generation to generation, creating what I call the family curse. Significant to me is that these characters are my ancestors, and they produced me. I am who I am because of their experiences, the good, the bad, and the ugly—every component of me. Consequently, their curse became mine, and they taught me how to mask emotional pain for the sake of others, even if it meant internally destroying myself.

It seems to be a common experience for people to bottle up their negative emotions and never address the pain they cause, all for another. However, the fact of the matter is, for this family, part of the family curse involves moving in mysterious ways that never allow others to know what we're thinking or how we truly feel. The story's characters all fall victim to the family curse, which is only encouraged by affiliation with religious beliefs, imposed by people with obscenities of their own inhibiting others' genuine authenticity. Throughout this story, I refer to these beliefs founded on unsupported life concepts as Authenticity Inhibitors.

Authenticity Inhibitors, or AI, references unsupported church legislation, which hindered many from being who God truly ordained them to be. With no valid biblical defense, man's opinions became the catalyst for many to develop an inability to be their authentically, God-ordained self. In many cases, we allow others to cover our mouths as we lack the strength to defend ourselves. This story's characters find themselves following a mask mandate imposed on them by others. Authenticity Inhibitors contribute to the brokenness of individuals who are mandated to follow said legislation. As a result of this individual brokenness, broken families are bred, which produces broken churches and provides the affluence needed to generate our communities' chaos.

In this book, I expose the emotional wreck that I became as I masked a concoction of emotions—developed from all the seeds planted by my ancestral influences. Additionally, Authenticity Inhibitors imposed by a particular people who used their religious power to control the minds and confiscate the freedom of me and many others, became the catalyst for my emotional instability. For this cause, I concealed those areas of my life where my true identity didn't fit the plan of what they expected me to be. However, by removing my mask, I identified my true identity and embraced genuine authenticity. This exposure allowed me to identify the toxicity of parts of my childhood reality, therefore realizing the chance to change the reflection of me that I dared not see. Consequently, I triumphantly overcome the family curse, taking strides to become all God created me to be.

In this book's conclusion, I speak to the unmasking process, where I provide the reader with the tools to remove the mask with Meditation, Affirmation, Salvation, and Knowledge. As we wear a physical mask today, to be safe from a virus we cannot see, many of us have exposed hidden hurt and pain that has bruised us emotionally. We cannot expect to reap or produce anything other than what is planted in us unless we take control of our lives and destroy the cycle of generational curses, ridding ourselves of others' negative influences. For the sake of our health and the unity of our communities, our hidden emotions must be uncovered, revealing our true selves as we journey toward unmasking.

CHAPTER 1

ALGIE'S FURY

Algie finds himself masking a deep-rooted emotion called fury for the sake of his self-image.

The telling of this story begins at a time before my mother met my father. The year was 1970, November 12 to be exact, and David Lloyd and Joyce Ann Evans brought a beautiful baby girl into the world, their first child, and they called her Darla Denise. She is my mother, and her story is how we begin examining the masks my family wore, for it's the decisions she made and her life's actions that led to my conception. So, indeed, telling my story can't be done without telling hers. Her story is one of insecurity and low self-esteem, a generational curse passed from the pains of the generations before.

To fully understand Darla, we must first journey together to western Alabama. Here we meet Algie Lee Evans, Jr., my great-grandfather. All knew Algie to be smooth and charismatic. Family accounts say that Algie was a ladies' man and had a mission to be with as many women as he could. I trace his story back to the Choctaw Nation, a tribe of artists, professionals, musicians, storytellers, innovators, leaders, athletes, warriors, and caregivers. Algie Jr.'s grandfather was a native of this nation, and his heritage can be traced well back into the early 1800s to a prosperous land with a flourishing people, bold, healthy, and courageous.

The Choctaw courage lasted through the mid-1800s, surpassing and surviving the Indian Removal said to have forced most Native Americans from their ancestral homelands in the eastern United States to lands west of the Mississippi River, landing many of them in Oklahoma. The Choctaw Nation's tribal records in western Alabama list where Algie Jr.'s father was born. The date was June 20, 1889, when Algie Lee Evans, Sr., was born in Bessemer, Alabama. In 1912, Algie Sr. married a woman by the name of Johnnie Mae Lawson. Historical records presume that her parents were slaves and that the surname Lawson was given to them as it was the name of their slave owners.

History says the Lawson name can be associated with the ancient Anglo-Saxon culture of Britain. History also tells us that thousands of English families fled England's unrest. Shortly after arriving in present-day America, they brutally took the lands of those native to it and shipped over people from the African continent to be slaves here. Native Americans, such as Algie Sr.'s ancestors, lost their land through force. Africans, such as Johnnie Mae's ancestors, were forced into slavery, exploited to work as indentured servants, and often given their enslavers' surname. Algie and Johnnie Mae's experiences, being displaced from their homes, became the seed of the first emotion unveiled—fury.

Few people would disagree that both Algie Sr. and Johnnie Mae have reason to be furious, having been ripped from their home and brutalized. The trouble came in that their current environment didn't allow for the expression of these emotions. History records that decades after slavery ended, people of color could lose their lives by speaking up to their white oppressors. Therefore, people of color found ways to mask their emotions simply to stay alive. The mask mandate, in their case, is life or death, literally.

These unaddressed emotions incubated and became a part of Algie Sr. and Johnnie Mae's emotional construct. They both lived in that fear-ridden state of fury, in which they raised their children as well. Born in varying eras of oppression and pain, each of their children faced some battle with this fury. It seems inevitable that the emotions derived from what their parents met would shape these children into what they became. Consequently, their environmental forces contributed to the entire construct of who the children became.

Algie Jr. is one of seven children born to Algie Sr. and Johnnie Mae. He was born March 11, 1914, in Alabama, and family accounts suspected that he may have taken his parents' pain the worst. Therefore, he reaped the results of the seed of fury pollinated by the experiences of his parents. Algie Jr. was a very stern, firm, and no-nonsense type of guy. He strived to be a hard worker and provider for his home, embodying his father's warrior, leadership, and caregiver principles. From his mother, Algie took perseverance and an ability to overcome adversity. He was quick-witted and was determined not to be destroyed by his environment. Nonetheless, despite all these excellent characteristics, Algie Jr. was furious.

Defined as extraordinarily wild and violently angry, Algie embodied fury derived from unfavorable encounters and negative experiences. As Algie Jr. matured, he faced countless damaging experiences, adding to his emotional construct. While slavery had ended, segregation had only begun. With his father's strength and his mother's wit, Algie had all the components of a dangerous emotional makeup, which was the catalyst for Algie's fury. This catalyst led to violent and destructive actions, sexual perversions, and immoral behaviors. Algie Jr. lived in a state of rage, making consecutive decisions leading him into a bottomless pit of despair.

Sources believe that Algie finally hit rock bottom in 1939 when suspicion arose that Algie and his brothers killed a white man for raping their sister. The Evans brothers scattered throughout southern America, all except for Algie Jr., who met a woman and her mother during this time. He used them as part of his escape plan from the South's chaos to a better life in the North's lands. Sarah Jane Lawton and her mother, Lelar Wimbley, posed as his slaves as a decoy to escape from Alabama to Michigan.

Moving to Michigan didn't change the fact that Algie Jr. was still furious. Sarah, however, came from a lineage of God-fearing people. They followed and believed in the laws of God's power. Lelar was a praying woman who found favor in the sight of God. Upon arriving in Michigan, Lelar joined the present-day landmark Clinton Street Greater Bethlehem Temple in Detroit. Lelar was known as a woman of faith with healing hands that she used to pray against the scarlet fever plague of that day.

Considering the faith of Lelar, the faith community would have Algie and Sarah be married if they were going to live together. With this faith, Lelar prayed, and Algie Jr. and Sarah were married on June 27, 1942. However, Algie Jr. still lived with emotional fury. Instead of addressing his emotional pain, he put on a mask used to disguise his internal struggle. In our community, including those of Black faith-based persuasions, healthy expression of male emotion was often discouraged.

AUTHENTICITY INHIBITOR #1

In our communities, men mustn't show any emotion. They must wield an iron fist that matches the strength of their position.

Stories like these are not uncommon in religious settings and churches. As we teach people to present themselves in religious piety, a child on the inside cries out for relief from the pain that developed from the misuse of their youth. It is because they perfected masking that pain that they even gained the position they have obtained. Trained to be a bishop, deacon, pastor, or another type of leader, their inner pain is so great that they perpetuate negativity on others in their care. These masked emotions often result in self-righteous behaviors that only breed continuous pain cycles for all who encounter these leaders.

Algie Jr. played the part of a man of God, hiding the fact that the things he experienced in his life had developed uncontrollable anger inside. His past sins were haunting him, making him more furious every day. His mask mandate was for his culture as he aimed to show no weakness, never letting anyone see his flaws. However, the danger of holding in emotions is, our minds, like a balloon, only have so much capacity for unresolved feelings. At some point, when that capacity exceeds, an explosion will occur. Additionally, as a plant continues to grow unless someone plucks up the root, unresolved emotions will grow through generations of people until we address those emotions.

We find where Algie's unresolved fury indeed exploded and continued to grow in his children's lives, beginning the family curse. Algie's children experience these furious explosions often, damaging the emotional construct of his children, who passed that pain to their children as well.

If we're honest, many of us have found ourselves in similar predicaments and are on the brink of explosive behaviors. Some of us are masking a fury-like emotion because we feel the need to be bold for the culture. Each of us has cultural influences that govern our way of life. However, some of those influences are toxic to our children and us. The idea that being a man exempts one from expressing emotions is unhealthy. Men, just like women, only have so much available capacity for unresolved feelings. As perpetuated in some churches, this cultural ideology regarding male emotions has been detrimental to many.

The mass incarceration of men, particularly men of color, affirms that this way of life is no way of life at all. Men who fail to express their emotions make mistakes that land them in jail or, worse, in a grave. Bottling up emotions is a common mistake made by many men who neglect to understand the importance of self-care. It is healthy to want to belong for the culture, but it is just as essential to address the hidden pains that have led us to our fury. When on a plane, the flight attendant reminds the passengers that in the event of cabin pressure failure, one ought to administer oxygen to themselves first and then help others around them. If more of us considered the need to help ourselves, fewer men would be in jail after making mistakes out of fury and would be free to be their authentic selves.

Algie never had the chance to be his authentic self as he died before having the opportunity. Before dying, though, he passed along the family curse through abuse, physically and emotionally. His abusive ways were a result of his inner pain, which developed his wrath and his fury. I imagine that if he had a chance to address his hurt adequately, his children might have avoided much of Algie's rage. Nonetheless, they now live with their pain and are faced with a choice: Will they choose to address this pain or mask it for the sake of the culture? If you identify with Algie, or maybe you think Algie was like your dad, you have a choice. Address the hurt within or leave it like an inheritance to your children. I chose freedom and authenticity; you can choose it too. We can leave our children with peace and not the emotional wreckage passed to Algie's children and then inevitably through generations to me.

CHAPTER 2

DAVID'S HATRED

David develops hatred in his heart as a result of the actions of his father.

The year was 1950, and Algie Jr and Sarah were about to have another child. His name was David Lloyd Evans, and he is my grandfather. The saying the apple doesn't fall too far from the tree is the epitome of what happened here. While David had a pretty normal childhood, he had many experiences that became the seeds that formed his emotional construct. A mutation of the fury emotion called hatred had now developed as a part of who David is. Much of this hatred was the direct result of the damage his father's explosive emotions created.

David found himself at the brunt end of his father's wrath, receiving at least one whipping a day. Algie's fury was out of control, which led him to be physically abusive and sexually immoral as well. David found himself often with his father when he would masquerade around the town, sowing his royal oats. These abusive childhood experiences and the encounters with sexual acts became seeds that further added to the construct of who David was. This combination awakened the emotion we address here, David's hatred.

Hatred is a powerful feeling of dislike, and David had much to dislike as he lived in a pattern of abuse. David developed a hatred for his father and his actions, and he later hated himself as he begins to reenact his father's decisions. David's father often threatened him that he could never tell of the acts he watched his father perform. Accordingly, David expressing his hatred toward his father and himself was not allowed. So, David put on a mask as well. His mask mandate was for his parents. David then lived in the same space as his father, hiding his inner struggles to please his father.

A continuum of this behavior continued until the day David had an encounter with Christ and had a Pentecostal experience in the early sixties. Fleeing from his father's ways and his toxic actions, David decided to join his sister and brother-in-law in Kenosha, Wisconsin. However, this is where we find out that even after an encounter with Christ, one must still address their past emotional trauma to be made entirely whole. Presumably, David was well, as he lived with a smile on his face, but this smile only masked the fact that he had an overwhelming distaste of his past pain. He no longer wore this mask to please his father; instead, he wore his mask to please the church's people. David did all he could to make "church folks" happy while battling inside with a warped mind from the family curse he inherited from his father. The seed of sexual perversion, planted there by his father, was not addressed throughout his life—not by the church, because, let's face it, we don't talk about sex in the church.

AUTHENTICITY INHIBITOR #2

The church holds that there's no need to discuss your desire for sex. Just don't do it until you're married; relieve your stress with a cold shower, at best.

One of the many taboo topics in the church house was sex, unless the preacher taught to abstain or don't do it. In many respects, we have been experts at explaining what man shouldn't do while failing at explaining why. Explaining why is just as essential as explaining the what, as the why explanation provides purpose to whatever one should or should not do. This purpose creates intentionality that helps one make an informed choice when faced with making a decision. When healthy conversations about sex derive from an unbiased, biblical perspective, people can view their sexual desires from a lens of knowledge and understanding and not fear and ignorance.

David's struggle with internal sexual desires, heightened by David's hatred for himself and others, was the next layer to the family curse. David not only had a hatred for his father but was beginning to hate the desires which dwelled within himself. Unfortunately, David didn't realize that his feelings weren't uncommon and that there was indeed a proper way to address them. The Bible tells us in Genesis, "It is not good that the man should be alone" (King James Version, Genesis 2:18). These words from God show us an understanding of man's natural desire for affection and the correlation of that affection with sex. We understand that the Scriptures identify fornication and adultery as sins. However, sex, in and of itself, is ordained by God. Therefore, there must be a proper way to engage in healthy conversations regarding sexual health.

Most fail to realize that once one performs sexual acts, they join themselves to that person's spirit. Paul asks the question in the Bible, "What? Know ye not that he which is joined to a harlot is one body?" (King James Version, 1 Corinthians 6:16). In most cases, the answer to this question is no. The lack of knowledge of why we abstain from multiple sexual partners contributes to widespread sexual immorality worldwide. When we address why one should avoid fornication without damaging the natural affection that one should have for the opposite sex, we allow for healthy premarital conversations about sex and healthy sexual behavior during the marriage. These failed conversations resulted in David joining together with many spirits that only fueled his self-hatred.

Additionally, we must remember that what a man sees also affects his ability to be sexually moral. The Gospel according to St. Matthew tells us, "Whosoever looketh on a woman to lust after her hath committed adultery with her already in his heart" (King James Version, Matthew 5:28). What one sees and looks at can create a dilemma for their heart. David had seen his father's immoral behavior and knew little about the godly way to engage in sexual acts. All he knew was his flesh desired it, and he wanted it at any cost. It was not good for him to be alone.

As he struggled with his sexual desires, David's self-hatred only increased, adding more layers to the emotional toll, the family curse. Some of us can relate to the emotional roller coaster David rode as he fought his fleshly urge for one sexual partner after another, often due to abuse from a parent or other loved one, suffering in silence, telling no one, and feeling unheard and misunderstood. Some of us have turned to others, maybe even people of a church. Instead of being helped, we've been appeased and not given proper support. Having no one to talk to out of fear that we'd be labeled unrighteous makes the struggle more difficult. One can't live an authentic life while living in hatred of themselves and fear of what others may think of them.

David's struggle continued through countless sermons reminding him that his thoughts were impure, never giving him a method by which he could overcome those thoughts and maintain the integrity of his natural affection. We can all relate to a time where our actions made us hate the very sight of ourselves in the mirror. This self-hatred if unaddressed is toxic to the point of self-destruction. Like David, those with self-hatred often overindulge and have no temperance, leading to various ailments. Besides an overindulgence in sex, David overate and found himself suffering from diabetes and other health ailments, which became a part of the remainder of his life.

David's hatred and resentment of all he faced in life prevented him from flourishing in Wisconsin. It seemed as if he couldn't settle with the weight of his past, which he always carried with him. The sins of his father had caused him to develop a lasting scar of hatred. The unfortunate thing is that these scars were now a spirit that became a part of the emotional construct for every woman he joined, adding new layers to the family curse. While the events of David's life continued to be unfavorable, he, too, had a choice. He could have struggled alone and carried the burden of internal conflict by himself, or he could have taken the opportunity to speak up and ask for the help that he needed.

David chose to run, returning to what was familiar, still carrying the weight of his past experiences, which haunted him. Like David, some of us are bearing the burdens of a traumatic family past that troubles us. Self-hatred has developed an inability for us to reject the notion that our heart's desires are uncontrollable. With proper knowledge and care for ourselves, we can be better than David and seek understanding and love ourselves despite what we've faced in our past. Unfortunately, David failed to address these traumas and dragged others into this chaos in his life, perpetuating the family curse.

David then joined a woman he procreated with, and the cycle continued. This woman then had to choose whether to reject the emotional baggage that came with David or ignore it to be with the man she loved. Do you identify with David? Maybe you identify as a woman disregarding the baggage that comes with the man you love. Well, you have a choice. Address that hurt within you, for if you continue ignoring it, it will undoubtedly be an inheritance to your children. The cycle then continued through David to his spouse, creating a path for this self-hatred through generations to me.

CHAPTER 3

JOYCE'S HEARTBREAK

Joyce experiences heartbreak leading to attempted suicide after David's infidelity.

The year was 1969, and David decided he should go back home to Detroit and try to survive his emotional instability there. Shortly after returning to Detroit, David was on one of his frequent rides home on the bus when he encountered a woman. She caught his attention, and he decided he would take his chance. During their conversation, they noticed that they had many mutual friends, and they had much in common; most of this commonality was the church. However, despite the many commonalities, one slight difference that could not go overlooked was embedded in their Pentecostal common ground.

The love story of these two reminds me of a modern-day religious Romeo and Juliet experience. David of the House of Apostolic and Joyce of the House of COGIC (Church of God In Christ), two slightly different Pentecostal movements, had an apparent disagreement. The rivalry was over the proper method for baptism. The Apostolic House believed that the church must explicitly profess Jesus's name in the baptism's verbiage. In contrast, The COGIC House conducted baptisms, doing so in "the Name of the Father, the Son, and the Holy Ghost", the Trinity vs. oneness.

The two families, specifically Joyce's mom, wanted nothing to do with their children coming together. Born December 2, 1946, Joyce was the daughter of James and Hazel Smith, two prominent COGIC reformation members. They wanted nothing but the best for their daughter, and dating an Apostolic man was out of the confines of their hopes. Joyce, however, wanted to be married, and she loved David. David was struggling in his flesh, and with the principle in hand, "It is better to marry than to burn," the two families put aside their differences, and David and Joyce were married before they ever really knew one another deeply.

After just a few exchange visits between each other's churches, David proposed to Joyce, and they were married in the year 1970 in Detroit, Michigan, just shy of a year later. The two knew very little about one another; all they knew is that they felt they loved one another. With the caregiver principle planted in him from his ancestors, David was able to assure Joyce that he would provide and care for her for all his days, and with the push of the church, the two felt the best thing to do was to marry.

AUTHENTICITY INHIBITOR #3

The church demands that you must marry in three to six months of dating, no exceptions; quickly propose, no consideration and no debating.

The Bible provides explicit instruction on what marriage should look like once entered into and how we should choose our spouse. However, the Scriptures offer very little education about how long one should deliberate on selecting their spouse. There are, however, clear consequences to marrying the wrong person as the Bible gives strict guidance on the sanctity of marriage and the provisions for getting out of it.

With this in mind, I refer to research conducted by the Barna Group. This company has completed more than one million interviews throughout hundreds of studies. It has become a go-to source for insights about faith and culture, leadership and vocation, and generations.

Barna's research says that 33% of those who identify as born-again Christians have experienced a divorce. Paul writes in one of his letters to the church at Corinth, "To the married, I give this command (not I, but the Lord): A wife must not separate from her husband. But if she does, she must remain unmarried or else be reconciled to her husband. And a husband must not divorce his wife" (New International Version, 1973/2011, 1 Corinthians 7:10–11). Considering these words, I would advise one to be very careful who they decide to marry. Once two persons make vows to one another, God's Word commands them to join for life. Why, then, might we force someone into a lifelong decision that has such extreme implications so hastily, especially without taking into account what a person has, whether they were ready or genuinely in love?

I believe the ideology of Authenticity Inhibitor #3 produced unnecessary strain on many marriages throughout time. Couples were required to choose between staying in a marriage where they despised their mate, living miserably, or divorcing from the union, accepting the implications as recorded in God's Word. Joyce and David were about to face these very unfavorable decisions as they hastened to the altar to make vows. The two wasted no time communing with one another, and nearly five days after "I do," the two conceived. While they were both excited to be parents, and both families were happy about the new baby to come, the family's rapid growth took a toll on this young marriage.

Conceiving a child, regardless of the circumstances, was considered a blessing. The church people didn't usually happily receive parents who displayed emotions other than joy and excitement about conceiving a child. Joyce and David showed that they were excited to be expecting a child, but David, who was still affected by his lack of stability and the wounds from his father, was only using this joy to mask his hidden emotions: self-hatred and now worry. David feared that he wouldn't be all that this child needed him to be, and no one could know how he felt about himself.

Some may wonder why they didn't wait to have children, maybe use contraception or other birth control. Indeed, various forms existed in the seventies. Well, the answer to that is it was considered a sin to do so.

AUTHENTICITY INHIBITOR #4

Birth control is prohibited in the church, for a married woman shall bear children until God says her womb has outlived its worth.

The church set a rule that there was no need for contraception because one should only use sex as a procreation method. While the Bible gives clear and direct guidance regarding the morality of many different topics, birth control isn't one of them. Therefore, any interpretations on the subject said to derive from the Bible are only opinions and not biblical evidence. It's an unfortunate reality to consider that people blindly adhered to rules like these, having children uncontrollably, all in the name of holiness. As a result, many had children outside of their means, financially, physically, and even mentally as they struggled in silence with battles in their mind.

One after the others, several children were born to Joyce and David as the Evans clan grew swiftly. Seemingly everything was well, but David's scars were too deep, and his uncontrollable desires made him weak. And so, Joyce's heartbreak happened for her eldest daughters to see. David succumbed to his sinful desires, and Joyce found out that there was another woman. Joyce couldn't believe that this was true, so she packed her children into a vehicle to confront the woman in question. This heartbreak led to a potentially irreparable event that could have changed the remainder of this story.

The year was about 1974, and tensions were at an all-time high in the Evans home. It was a hot summer day, and Joyce was doing laundry and caring for the house when she found a receipt for flowers purchased for that other woman. Joyce confronted David, and he denied involvement. With suspicion of the truth of David's words, Joyce packed her eldest daughters in the car and headed to the shipping address on the receipt. Joyce, Darla, and Angela all traveled to Detroit, Michigan, where the woman lived. After arrival, Joyce decided to confront the other woman as to who she was. After this confrontation, Joyce received assurance that indeed David was having an affair.

With tears in her eyes and a broken heart, Joyce returned to her car and began to drive. With her heartbreak exposed, this encounter planted that seed that could have altered the entire course of this story. Indeed, the seed planted was a seed of suicide. Joyce made a stop and bought candy for both Darla and Angela and said to them, "Mommy loves you both so very much." They all returned to the car, the children not knowing what Joyce had planned. The pain felt from betrayal coupled with the rage of hatred had left Joyce with no will to live.

With her children in the car, Joyce began to drive east toward the lake, a favorite spot for the children. Little did they know this would be a visit to the lake like none other. Joyce, overcome by her heartbreak, pressed on the gas at high speed with the intent to drive into the lake, ending it all. It was the screams of her children and the grace of God that just before making it to the lake, Joyce stopped and came to herself. Joyce never spoke of that encounter again.

Instead, she masked her hurt for the sake of her children and returned home to her husband.

This encounter became the pivotal point that aided in distributing the family curse to the next generation. Fury and sexual immorality, self-hatred and fear, heartbreak and suicidal thoughts became various layers of this generational curse that was the mantle passed throughout generations of Evans people. In front of her children, Joyce's heartbreak experience became a traumatic event that her children wrestled with throughout their lives. Like Joyce, some have been in relationships that have pushed them to the brink of ending their lives—wondering if after uncontrollable heartbreak there is any reason to continue living.

If you identify with Joyce, I want you to remember that you have a choice. As long as we continue to bottle up those emotions inside and hide them from others, we will never be able to overcome them. You owe it to yourself to choose yourself. It is okay to care for yourself and decide that your well-being is important too. Holding on to those emotions will only breed a place for self-harm. Don't allow someone else's actions to be your ruin. It would be best if you heal, or consequentially, you'll pass that pain to the ones you love the most. Joyce returned to David despite the affair, and they continued married to one another, never addressing the emotional toll they both experienced. The family cycle continued through their children as they passed along this toxic heartbreak through generations to Darla and, in time, to me.

CHAPTER 4

DARLA'S INSECURITY

Darla develops insecurities resulting from her father's mistakes which led to her mother's mishaps.

As the world turned and time continued, Darla entered her teenage years and developed adverse reactions to her childhood experiences. Traumatic experiences have a way of manifesting into various types of emotions. In this case, Darla's traumatic experiences of seeing her father's mistakes and her mother's potential missteps manifested into Darla's insecurities. These insecurities developed toxic ideologies of how men should treat women and how women should respond to a man's mistreatment. From these insecurities, Darla began looking for love in all the wrong places.

Most mental health professionals would suggest family counseling after traumatic experiences such as these. However, seeking counsel from a "shrink" has a negative stigma in the community and the church.

AUTHENTICITY INHIBITOR #5

Seeking help from a mental health professional is prohibited in the church. One should only seek God for guidance and their pastor for counseling here on Earth.

Unfortunately, church culture demonized the mental health profession so intently that some have had help right in front of them that they couldn't receive. Some pastors and leaders have stood in between trained professionals' God-given abilities only to please their egos. Pride would make a man with little to no knowledge or expertise on a topic insist that another come only to them for guidance in that area. Most understand that a pastor is looking to protect the people they lead, but where does this protective nature blur the lines with oppressive behaviors that do more damage than good and potentially interfere with God's plan in the lives of His people?

Darla suffered through the emotional turmoil of insecurities. Darla's uncertainty and anxiety about herself and her lack of confidence developed these insecurities. Additionally, the near-death experience and Darla's knowledge of her father's actions were enough to cause anyone to have some battles in their mind. Unfortunately, Joyce is hiding the fact that she is fighting with heartbreak in her mind, David is entertaining his conflicts, and Darla feels unheard and alone. With pure intentions but misguided actions, no one got the help they needed, and people suffered.

Darla, loved by her grandparents, parents, aunts, and uncles, unknowingly contained seeds planted by her experiences and encounters. It doesn't matter how loved you are by those around you; when you are insecure about who you are, you will have difficulties receiving others' love or knowing what real love is. This concept is shown throughout the life of Darla as she overcompensated to feel accepted by others. Darla hid these feelings with ease as she had everything she wanted and needed materialistically. Despite David's internal struggles, he was always a hardworking provider for his family; he loved his children.

In addition to David's love for his children, his mother instilled in him to love the church as well. Darla's insecurities created a belief that maybe David loved the church more than he loved her. David served the people of God in the media broadcast ministry, technology support ministries, and many other auxiliaries of help across the church. David was beloved of many, and to this day, many speak fondly of him and his personality. Joyce also loved the church and served alongside her husband to support the ministry, overseeing the Vacation Bible School for children in the church and the surrounding community.

David and Joyce were faithful supporters of the ministry, making Darla and her siblings a part of the premier church group called preacher's kids. Many believe that some prestige comes from being a part of this group. However, there is also so much turmoil that comes with the territory. Darla and her siblings spent much of their family time at the church. Family vacations consisted of attending the church conventions. There was little to no time for family gatherings, and the church became their family. This way of life was the culture of the time, and no one questioned it. It was welcomed by all and supported as the tradition.

With this tradition, where the church took over every aspect of their lives, Darla's self-esteem continued to dwindle even at home. Joyce was a wonderful mother and would prepare full-course meals for the family. One particular day, Joyce was preparing a meal: smothered pork chops, greens and smoked neck bones, mac and cheese, and something sweet to eat and drink. Joyce had the table spread, everyone was around the table to eat, and Joyce began making everyone's plate. Everyone was waiting to dig in as the aroma made everyone's mouth water. Joyce was plating the last serving. It was Darla's plate, but it wasn't the dinner prepared for everyone else. For Darla, Joyce plated a salad.

Joyce's intentions, believed to have been pure, created another traumatic experience for Darla. Joyce couldn't see how such isolation could be traumatic to her daughter, as her present emotional dysfunction blinded her. Darla was utterly embarrassed in front of the entire family, but she hid this as she carried the burden of her pain in silence throughout her entire childhood. This trauma emboldened Darla's insecurities as she hoped someone would love her just the way she was. Growing up sheltered from the world and alone in her heart, Darla had no real idea of what love was.

Muzzled by the mask she wore to protect the family name and their image in the church, Darla learned to play the part. However, she lived a life that wasn't real to be the person the church thought she should be. In reality, behind her mask was a host of insecurities, pain, and hurt. These emotions, coupled with the feelings of fury, hatred, and heartbreak, passed from her ancestors. Darla was unstable and looking for love in all the wrong places. Darla sought this love in school, but her differences made that difficult to find, not merely because of their way of life but also because of the way they dressed.

AUTHENTICITY INHIBITOR #6

Women of the church shall not wear any other lower garment but a skirt, which must cover their ankles and be unfitted. They must not participate in any activity or sport where any other attire is required; if they do, they have committed sin.

The appearance of women in the church seemed to be a hot topic all over the body of Christ. Unfortunately, some wouldn't even fellowship a church that allowed "their women" to adorn themselves in jewelry or makeup, even in modesty. The "men of God" would consider a woman who wore a pair of pants to have sinned against God. Struggling with insecurities about their appearance, countless women braced themselves for mean and nasty opinions of people who professed to be godly, all over a tradition that had no real biblical defense. Some even were forced into a masked emotional situation of isolation.

In this isolated place, many dissolved friendships and even family relationships at the word of traditional leadership. This isolation, masked as the pastor's effort to protect people from harm, was considered the sanctification required for church members. However, pride and ego created a will to separate from those who only disagreed on the definition of modesty. While seemingly well-intended, this isolation was misguided. It was a contributor to the catalyst that led to the masked reality of insecurities that we find in the lives of many men and women alike. The unfortunate cause of this reality is that those leaders are masking pain and desire of their own.

For Darla, her desire was simply to be loved. Darla's peers often ridiculed her, calling her "Skirt Girl." Being a little thicker than most girls her age, Darla endured additional ridicule from her classmates and blamed Authenticity Inhibitor #6 for this. There was little physical activity allowed for Darla since she couldn't dress the part. They would receive letters from the church excusing them from gym class, stating the dress code was against their faith. Darla couldn't show her pain and resentment because the preacher's kids can't have any woes. "Don't you dare let them see you cry! You're an Evans; hold your head up high!" These sayings of David, which he learned from his father, quickly taught Darla how to become an alternate personality when in the church's presence.

David's continued indiscretion caused Joyce and David to divorce. David ensured his children got the best of education, private education at that. But regardless of the great schools they attended, Darla could not escape the painful feeling of humiliation and distress caused by her father's wrongdoing. The irrational choices her father made planted the seed that developed into Darla's shame. David continued to provide for his children, but his unresolved emotions coupled with his infidelity were too much for Joyce to handle. These irreconcilable differences sent Joyce and David on two different paths for several years.

So many can identify with the feeling of insecurity and emotional abandonment that Darla experienced. If you are a preacher's kid, you may even identify with the need to hide your feelings for the sake of the family name. Doing so led Darla into a deep place of insecurity, and she then made choices that led to other emotions. These choices added to the family curse's construct as the family cycle continued, passing these insecurities to me. Possibly, you've masked your insecurities for the sake of the family name. You have a choice. Making the wrong choice could lead to choices that produce shame.

CHAPTER 5

DARLA'S SHAME

Darla couples her insecurities with shame after a public humiliation.

As the oldest child of six, Darla saw all her father's actions. However, he taught her to cover for his indiscretions, especially for the church folks. "What happens in this house, stays in this house" were David's words, which became the Evans home's mantra. Very few will admit it, but many upheld this mantra in most of their homes. Everyone would come together in the church house to lift the name of Jesus, only to return home to the chaos developed from acts of infidelity or other immoralities or abuse taking place in their homes. As a result, the tensions derived from these toxic relationships affect both the main characters and everyone who surrounded them.

After Joyce and David's separation, David met a man I refer to as Preacher. David, who was looking to address his past demons, endeavored to reclaim himself to God. He desperately wanted to address his inner hurt. However, it was Preacher's understanding that a man couldn't go to God for himself. Preacher's role was to help David get to God.

David reclaimed himself to the church and devoted himself to Preacher, not necessarily to the ministry of God. David and Preacher began a church I will refer to as Hopkins Street. This church became a breeding ground for Darla's shame and the petri dish that grew the family curse.

AUTHENTICITY INHIBITOR #7

God shall not speak to just any man, saved or unsaved; God only engages with the pastor God has put in place.

To date, we find pastors who believe that God only speaks to them. However, God can and does talk to all people. We all belong to Him, and while having spiritual guidance and leadership is imperative, it does not change the fact that God can use and speak to any of us at His discretion, and He needs no intermediary. The notion that God only has one type of person on Earth that He communicates through is unfounded in God's Word. Even those who find themselves in an error of God's Word can hear the voice of God and be available to be used of Him. Being out of God's will is not a place any man should desire to be, but God still loves us even there.

Through the story of Christ, the Word of God provides humanity with a connection to God and not solely through the pastor. John writes in the Bible, "My little children, these things write I unto you, that ye sin not. And if any man sin, we have an advocate with the Father, Jesus Christ the righteous" (King James Version, 1 John 2:1). We must be careful not to allow our pride and arrogance about our church positions to cause us to forget we are only stewards of God's Word through His Son. "For God so loved the world, that he gave his only begotten Son, that whosoever believeth in him should not perish, but have everlasting life" (King James Version, John 3:16). Christ, the righteous, He without sin, is our Savior and Advocate.

Indeed, an offender of God's laws has created separation from God, and for that, God's judgment may be upon them. However, if a person falls into sin, Christ makes intercession for them without the need of another. We can go to Christ as the Bible says, "Let us, therefore, come boldly unto the throne of grace, that we may obtain mercy, and find grace to help in time of need." (King James Version, Hebrews 4:16). The Word of God reminds us that not only is our God a righteous judge, He is also very forgiving, and His mercy and compassion endureth forever. "It is of the Lord's mercies that we are not consumed because His compassions fail not" (King James Version, Lamentations 3:22).

It is by the grace of God that our sins have not consumed us. Nonetheless, an abundance of grace doesn't permit us to continue our sins, expecting His grace will always prevail. However, if we fall and need grace in our lives, the Word of God gives us an Advocate for that grace. David lived his life not honestly knowing how important the grace of God was. He lived his life through the trust of people in the church. When a person puts their faith in a man, the trusted man's mistakes or sins can ruin the truster's ability to believe.

After about a year of being back in the church, David returned to Michigan to reconcile his marriage with Joyce, and they remarried. Shortly after remarrying, Joyce, David, and their children, except Darla, moved to Milwaukee and lived with Preacher and his family in the Hopkins Street Ministry's apartments. Darla stayed in Detroit and moved in with her grandmother. After living with Grandma Hazel for a short while, Darla moved in with an aunt who exposed her to various forms of sexual promiscuity. There are few things more dangerous than a young adult with low self-esteem having exposure to their sexual desires, and this combination of things led to the many decisions that Darla made leading up to my conception and her shame.

Her choices began when Darla visited her parents and siblings in Milwaukee. Besides the Evans family and Preacher's family, another gentleman, a native of Chicago, lived in the lower residence and was a custodian for the church. Darla, who desired to be loved, cared for, admired, and sought after, sought someone to see her. She wished for someone confident to fill the void she had within—the emptiness of her father's presence and love in her early life.

Darla's desires led her to my father, the custodian in the Hopkins Street Ministry's lower residence. Beyond his work for the church, he was a musician. The man could sing and play the guitar like none other. People would come from all over to hear him play. Some say that he played so well that it seemed his guitar would talk. It was as if he brought the music to life. He was charming, charismatic, and a lady pleaser. As fate would have it, this man, my father, met Darla, my mother. In the middle of the day, David and Darla came to the front of Hopkins Street, and here is where my father, Marshall Benjamin Pope, known as Pope, met Darla for the first time.

David said, "Deedee," (this is what they called Darla) "meet Pope." Darla masked her thoughts of him and declared that she was in no way interested. However, the next Sunday after service, they met again at the Evans family's traditional Sunday dinner with the Hopkins Street Church members. Preacher's wife would cook soul food extraordinaire, and the tradition was that they all would break bread together on Sunday after worship. Pope's smooth, charming, and elusive ways caught the attention of Darla. He wanted her; she declared she didn't want him, but his confidence and persistence broke her down.

After trouble erupted in the aunt's home where Darla lived, she moved to Milwaukee permanently. After this move, Darla let her guard down and allowed herself to be vulnerable to Pope, and at one of those traditional Sunday dinners, she obliged the request of Pope for a date. Immediately following the feast, they both rode their bikes to Lake Michigan. They shared drinks, had a casual conversation, and enjoyed each other's company. The night was perfect, and Darla and Pope began courting.

Pope being twelve years older than Darla made him a bit more knowledgeable about relationships. He knew what moves to make and what buttons to push. Pope spoke to her desire for love, telling her she was pretty, complimenting her weight as beautiful, and assuring her that his passion was all for her. Darla felt that he cared for her and loved her, and for that, she loved him. After returning home together, Pope planned to make his move—behind the baptismal pool, of all places.

There they stood behind the baptismal site, and Pope moved in to plant a kiss, but before he could land the kiss, two of Darla's siblings came in and interrupted. The sibling interruption ruined their plans for that evening, but it didn't stop Darla and Pope from seeing one another again. Time and opportunity aligned in one of those times that they met, and from that meeting, Darla and Pope conceived.

With fear and concern, Darla realized her cycle's characteristics had not come that month and she might be pregnant. She went to the clinic for a test, where the nurse affirmed that Darla was pregnant. The nurse laid out all the options of how the story could go, even an option that would end my life sooner than anyone could've ever known she was pregnant. Ashamed and confused by the information she received, Darla weighed all the options, including the thought of aborting me. Pope was allowed in the room and given the news; he was seemingly unmoved. Pope's calm and peace were enough to place Darla's mind at ease, so they decided to band together and keep me.

For nearly four months, no one else knew that my story had begun. By the fourth month, Darla couldn't hide the pregnancy any longer. Joyce found out, and like Hazel, who had wanted nothing to do with David having her daughter, Joyce wanted nothing to do with Pope and Darla being together. After Joyce confronted Pope, an argument began, heard throughout the complex, including Preacher in the apartment across the hall. Once Preacher knew, he handled it in a way that developed Darla's shame.

AUTHENTICITY INHIBITOR #8

If one commits fornication in the church, and definitely when a child they've conceived, they must immediately be silenced or disfellowshipped publicly, in a meeting where all the saints can see.

It was a common tradition of holiness churches to conduct a meeting of correction called a Saints' Meeting. In these meetings, leaders told members' sins aloud, and those who sinned were silenced and disfellowshipped, or excommunicated from the church. Their names were often displayed on a list for all to see that they were longer in good standing with the church. Unfortunately, these actions became breeding grounds for shame and relentless pain unnecessarily inflicted by people who took joy in these actions—often taking pleasure in bringing judgment that God never intended. Leaders who run out of grace before God does concern me. The lack of wisdom used in these types of public humiliation can only come from a place of pride and misguidance.

Historically, in the Word of God, Old Testament writing shows where public atonement for sin, by way of animal sacrifice, was required as a part of reconciliation with God. Christ, however, came and became the ultimate sacrifice for humanity's sins in the world. Therefore, not only can one seek Christ for grace when they fall, but one is also not obligated to display their sacrifice for all to see publicly. The life we live will be that sacrifice. The humiliation and shame method, brought upon Darla in a meeting of the saints, did more damage than good.

Nonetheless, in that Saint's Meeting, Preacher read the words written to the Hebrews, according to God's Word, "Marriage is honourable in all, and the bed undefiled: but whoremongers and adulterers God will judge" (King James Version, Hebrews 13:4). Preacher continued in front of the saints to say, "All fornicators shall go to hell and burn for eternity . . . Sister Darla and Brother Pope have been having sex, and now the sister is pregnant." Preacher continues, providing the saints with details of the two's encounter for all who were in the congregation to hear. He ends by saying, "Tonight, I'm silencing them; they are not to take part in any matters of the church."

One might suggest that Preacher was within his right to remove them from their work in the church but imagine being Darla or Marshall, sitting in that church pew, being made a public spectacle to the entire congregation. Humiliation, shame, embarrassment, and hurt were all emotions that Darla felt sitting in that meeting. She couldn't believe that he had told the whole church what had happened to her. Darla resented her mother for confronting Pope and her father for not defending her. Additionally, she was angry with Pope for his part in this and herself for letting it happen. Still, Darla used the family's abilities to hide their emotions for the family name's sake.

Identifying with this type of public humiliation is more common than you might think. Darla's story is all too familiar in churches all over. These practices derived from misguided intention have been the hurt and ruin of so many throughout time. If you find yourself identifying with these experiences and emotions, I remind you that you have a choice. You can decide to own that mistake, reminding yourself that God has given you an opportunity for redemption since you are alive. Don't allow the shame of your action and others' impositions on you to be to your destruction.

If you find yourself acknowledging alignment with Darla's shame and insecurities, you too can be free. Acknowledgment of these hidden emotions of embarrassment and guilt is the first step to beginning the journey toward unmasking. You can decide today that you don't want to sit like a ticking time bomb on the verge of explosion, suffering in silence. Darla chose to bottle it up, and from that choice, the family cycle of emotional dysfunction layered the family curse all the more. From this dysfunction, Darla fell into a deep depression.

CHAPTER 6

DARLA'S DEPRESSION

Darla becomes depressed, trying to hold in the distress of her insecurities and shame.

As several months passed since the public shaming experience, Darla held resentment for the church and her family, which left her isolated with her thoughts. After some time, Preacher decided to restore Darla to fellowship with the church. Pope had yet to return to the church and was then active in a life of riotous living. As if the matter couldn't get any worse, Preacher received news that would be a bombshell to the Darla–Pope love story. Before sharing the information with Darla, Preacher shared the news with David, her father.

Remember that Pope was charming, charismatic, and a lady pleaser. No one knew just how much of a professional he was. Darla was about to find out the true nature of who Pope was. Preacher called a meeting with David and Darla. David arrived first but was not in the room when Darla came. Darla was shocked to see only Preacher there until David appeared from the restroom. David told Deedee to take a seat. Darla does as he requested nervously, and then

Preacher said, "Daughter, we found some troubling news. Pope is married."

Yes, my father was married, estranged from his wife for over three years, but he was still married. For the sake of anonymity, we will call her Gwen. Gwen wanted to be with Pope, but he wanted nothing to do with her. She found out that he had moved on and wanted to do everything she could to ruin that. Gwen had three children of her own, and two of them were Pope's. Darla confronted Pope about the news she received, and he told her that it's over, but she wouldn't let him be. "She won't sign the papers and divorce me." So Darla decided to leave him and allow him time to sort things out with his wife.

Things would only worsen when Gwen decided that she and her three children would move to Milwaukee and attend church at Hopkins Street. From the moment Gwen arrived until the moment she left; Darla's depression continued to worsen. Gwen had access to consistent money streams, which allowed her to pay bills for the church, sponsor shopping trips with the sisters, flash cash before Pope, and use that money to buy friendships. Darla felt betrayed by the sisters for receiving Gwen over her, knowing the dynamics of the matter. Depression set in as Darla fought to continue for the seed that she bore. My life was being developed in the womb while all this was taking place. Indeed, I was there while all this was happening; voiceless, but I was there.

Depression is said to cripple one's ability to function, let alone in pregnancy. So as Gwen's presence persisted for quite some time, Darla struggled to live for the sake of me in her womb. The final act of Gwen's time in Milwaukee was the service where she stood up to testify, and her testimony went like this:

"Praise the Lord Saints," she said.

"Praise the Lord," the saints responded.

Gwen testified, "I want to thank all the saints for being so nice to me while I was here, but I have to go now. I tried to work things out with my husband, but it just ain't working, and it has nothing to do with Darla either." Gwen left toward the church's double doors and turned to Darla and said, "You can have him now." Here is where that ticking time bomb exploded, and a fight erupted, only to be quickly broken up by David.

Shortly after this encounter, while in the church's basement, Darla's water broke. After being rushed to the hospital, Darla found that her firstborn was soon to come. It seemed as if I was in no rush to enter this world. Darla's labor took so long that Preacher, David, and Pope left to finish a construction job in Chicago. Darla encouraged him to go because she needed the money with a baby coming into the world. The time had come, and the baby boy began to crown. Darla started to push, Joyce by her side, and after a couple of big pushes, Darla delivered a healthy baby boy, 8 pounds, 15 ounces and 27 inches long—Bryan David Evans.

After about a year after the birth of Bryan, Darla and Pope reunited. Pope made promises that he would change his life and devote himself to Darla. During this time, she conceived again, and in search of a fresh start, Pope and

Darla moved from Milwaukee to Detroit, where they stayed in Grandma Hazel's home. During one of Grandma Hazel's morning prayers, she declared that Pope and Darla needed to marry, and they did. On December 26, 1992, in the living room of Grandma Hazel, they were married, and shortly after that, Jordan Lloyd Pope was born.

David was wroth after hearing that not only had his daughter had another child but that she and Pope had got married. Tensions rose between David and Darla because of this pregnancy, and he scolded Darla. However, David's hypocrisy in scolding Darla was bold in that he had a baby of his own on the way, and this baby wasn't Joyce's. Darla and Pope moved back to Milwaukee shortly after Jordan's birth, and later that year, David's second son is born.

After returning to Milwaukee, things seemed to be going well. Pope had aspirations and goals he was working to accomplish. He was living for God, and his passion for music was opening doors for him to instruct and teach. Pope was technology savvy and gifted in electronics and repair. In fact, in the neighborhood where we lived, he was known to be the guy who could fix just about anything. Pope was working to provide for his family and make an honest living; Darla and Pope even conceived two additional children Melodie Rose and Jasmyn Re'Joyce Pope. Unfortunately, there was a dangerous culture on Hopkins Street that caused many families to suffer.

AUTHENTICITY INHIBITOR #9

Bring all your money to the storehouse, no matter what your financial struggle at your house. God will provide for your whereabouts, all your needs, your children, and your spouse.

The principles of giving in the Word of God are clear. They admonish us to give liberally of our abundance and to tithe of our increase. Unfortunately, some use these godly principles to guilt-trip others into giving beyond their means. Those with much survive, and those with little continue to die. Many were providing money for power and prestige, leaving some families with their homes empty. For Pope, the cares of life and the pressure to keep up with the church's demands, I believe, turned him back to selling drugs.

One night, while Darla was cleaning the bathroom of their home, she found a vial. Not knowing what it was, she took it to her father to find out. David told her that they were drugs, and he took them and flushed them down the toilet. Pope became quite angry after finding his stash of drugs discarded. These events led to a pattern of very abusive behavior toward Darla, both physically and emotionally. This abusive behavior continued for several years as their children grew to see this abuse for themselves.

Birthed from shame and pain, Bryan was born into this family that had yet to address the emotional trauma that created the family curse. By that time, the entire cocktail of emotional dysfunction had been stirred, and unfortunately, it was in the bottle for Bryan to drink. Now it was Bryan's turn to take on the family mantle and live an emotionless life of trauma—trauma that he didn't choose but was awakened to by the inevitable events in his life. Darla could see his pain and his struggle, and this only deepened her depression.

Many erratic behaviors proved her depression to have worsened, but Darla's depression isn't what this story is all about. This story is about me. I am Bryan, and the family curse perpetuated as I grew older and life's traumatic experiences overcame me.

However, this is where it ends! The story tells of the trauma I faced and the pain I felt throughout life, but that part will only be the beginning. The unmasking is the climax of the story where I expose myself to the world to be vulnerable enough the get the freedom that I needed. Algie, David, Joyce, Darla, and even Pope are characters that contributed to my totality; my arrival was because of them. However, how I lived my life would be because of me. Even though I started allowing the family plan to consume me initially, I decided to live my life authentically before the end.

CHAPTER 7
BRYAN'S EXPOSURE

Bryan arrives into a world of unresolved emotions, which exposes him to the family curse of emotional instability.

Have you ever wondered why you do some of the things you do? I did, and I concluded that we are the sum of the seeds planted in us by those that created us. These seeds were planted and multiplied throughout our lives, establishing perpetual cycles that became the construct of our reality. For me, those cycles were of hurt and pain, producing several emotional dysfunction mutations for years to come. Few people knew I was battling with the family curse because this family taught me to be the master of disguise. There were many disguises in our home, necessary to protect the family name and our status in the church. I could show no hurt or pain because showing weakness was not a part of who we are.

Who are we? We are Evans's, and we are the founding members of the Hopkins Street Church; what joy. My grandfather, David, had forced us to be migrants from Michigan, and internally, this was not where I wanted to be. I was merely wearing a disguise to please Preacher and honor the family name. However, my actual reality was that I desired to be allowed to be a kid. I wished to have fun in school, go to prom, homecoming, and see a simple movie. I wanted to be allowed to enjoy both life and God. *But this city of God is odd, and I want to be out.*

This church inhibited my authenticity by requiring that I choose education or God.

> They set standards that are impossible for anyone to meet, especially me with all my flaws, God. I am now praying to be free of the unsubstantiated rules and regulations that have not come from you, God. They have developed from another man's plan, with no idea that the people are suffering at his hand's actions. With no other option but to do what Preacher has told my family to be right, I've put on this mask to hide who I am in front of them—only to develop a life of insecurity and hypocrisy, and now I don't even recognize myself. I wear this mask to hide my imperfection and pain because they told me being vulnerable isn't something I have the privilege of being, but this pain is real. My life's struggles have left infected scars from years of mismanagement.

Algie's fury, David's hatred, Joyce's heartbreak, and Darla's insecurities, shame, and depression were all seeds that lay within, growing and thriving. Hopkins Street was the perfect toxicity for fertilizing these seeds. With an unbalanced approach to living for God, the souls of men suffered and were never indeed cultivated to be the authentic persons God intended. Instead, many had a form of godliness but denied the real power of authenticity. As my ancestors' seeds grow in me, I had no actual ability to reject fear and embrace confidence. This lack of confidence traces back to when I was very young.

This lack of self-esteem, triggered by an occasion that I vividly remember, was the substance that began my emotional dysfunction. I vividly remember the first time I saw a dad drop off their child at school. I was in kindergarten, Mrs. Kushner's class, Benjamin Franklin Elementary School. I remember thinking, I wish I had a dad. I asked myself, *Why doesn't my dad love me? What did I do that made him leave?* All I wanted was to have him as a part of my life, to hear him call me son. I was too young to realize that he was battling an ailment to which he was losing the battle, and indeed it wasn't really about me. But that void became a part of me, and then every man I saw reminded me that he was not there.

But I can't show this! I feel like I had to be the strength for my siblings and the rock for my mom, so I covered this pain with strength, wit, and a smile. No one knew that secretly I was a wreck. I was wondering when he would find the strength to fight and come back to us, hoping every day that this would be the day he would say, "I'm coming home for good." Day after day, I wished that he'd return home for good. But my wish seemed to be impossible as he had by then made the drug house his home. He was too preoccupied with getting his next fix to be concerned with whether we had food in the fridge. For him, he was home.

Admittedly, this seemed unbearable, but with my mom's strength and my grandparent's support, I felt everything would be all right. Everything was okay until the first time I can ever remember the feeling of embarrassment. I was on the tot lot, being a child and enjoying the weather with my classmates around. From the corner of my eye, I spotted a man that walked by, and indeed it was him. Looking back, I realized he was high, but it didn't matter. I thought the day had finally come that he was coming home for good. As I approached the fence, two teachers and a guard snatched me away and yelled at him, telling him he could not stay.

I screamed, and I kicked, wondering, *What do they mean? Finally, Daddy has come to take me home for good.* I know now that my mother had an order against him; she decided for me that he didn't need to see me. I found myself overwhelmed with emotion. I was hoping to go home with him for good. I understood that his actions were of his own doing, but that didn't matter to me. He was my dad, and I wanted him home.

Because of that encounter, the school was on high alert. An adult accompanied me as an escort everywhere I went. They assumed he would come back and take me away. It was then, as a five-year-old kindergartener, that I experienced the embarrassment that the man I wanted to return home was, in my mom's eyes, a bad man who would hurt me. Conflicted in my mind, I tried to make sense of it by suppressing my emotions to get by. Getting by was made easy as long as I had a distraction to help with suppressing my feelings.

My distraction of choice was learning. I loved going to school and soaking up every bit of knowledge I possibly could. I believe now this was God ordained to prepare me how He would use me later in my life. I frequently asked why, but unfortunately, asking why at the Hopkins Street Church was not allowed.

AUTHENTICITY INHIBITOR #10

You don't ask the preacher why; fall in line, ensure that you have aligned with whatever the pastor designs as divine, and don't dare define anything other than that within this church's confines.

I was only a kid, inquisitively seeking to know how things worked. I was hoping to glean knowledge and understanding about why things were the way they were; however, this zeal to learn disrespected the church, and so my distraction from my pain was dissolved. I was too young to question what the church had at work. I was to do as told, exactly as described, and immediately when demanded. Even though I meant no disrespect with my question about the church, Preacher took offense.

I had embarrassed the family name, and David would ensure I was embarrassed as well. While my brother Jordan got a great majority of the whippings David handed out, I got my fair share as well. After embarrassing the family name, the post-service whipping was one of the first times I can remember chastisement publicly, and as a result, fear was coupled with my embarrassment.

The family did what Preacher said with no questions and no mind of their own. Questioning things that involved me was considered disrespectful, especially at my age. Unfortunately, however, I had difficulty not questioning others' intentions, especially when I could see the hypocrisy in their actions. The mantra "Do as I say and not as I do" became a way of life. Unfortunately, not only was it a way of life, but it was a culture that Preacher established in the Hopkins Street Church—leaving young people absent a voice to request understanding, advice, and guidance. After having their voices silenced, these young people went from not only having missing voices to being absent from church as well.

With my voice silenced, I can again hear the loud gaping scream of the pain resulting from my father's absence. I imagined that had he been there, maybe things would not have been as they were, with me overcome with embarrassment. But he was not there, and I was embarrassed about simply being who I am, inquisitive. So, to fit in the environment where I spent most of my life, I went along to get along. I embraced the family curse and placed on a mask, hiding who I am so that I pleased them. They desired that I fall in line with their traditions and concepts as described by these authenticity inhibitors. I nor others around me could be authentically ourselves. Instead, we conformed to the Hopkins Street way, according to the Hopkins Street people's mantra, that some things you'll only see on Hopkins Street.

I assumed a Hopkins Street Church member's role, learned their ways, actions, and sayings, and learned to camouflage among their customs and traditions, many of which had no factual biblical basis. Preacher led the church, and he made all the rules. Failure to comply with his laws would land you kicked out of the church and maybe even your name plastered on a board for all to see that you were no longer apart of this church. Sometimes I wondered whether Hopkins Street was no church at all, but rather a cult. Indeed, it was a religious system of adoration and devotion directed toward Preacher, masked as devotion to God, but this environment was toxic. For the sake of the family name, I toed the line just to fit in, and my reality became one of hypocrisy.

This hypocrisy had everyone thinking that everything within me was all right, but I was an emotional wreck inside. These emotions, exposed through traumatic experiences in school, were about to begin my breaking. It was the fourth grade at Congress Elementary School; I was a transfer. I still harbored fear and hurt from my childhood experiences, and I entered the classroom, new to the school, and everyone stared. I remember the boy who shouted from the back of the room, "What do you have on?" With no response to provide and fear in my eyes, the class began to laugh. Now, Darla's insecurities were a part of my present reality. I was self-conscious, and I didn't particularly appreciate how I looked. I spent many of my days with no self-confidence, as my classmates teased my lack of brand-named things.

But on my face, I wore a smile, brushing off the fact that I was hurt.

Hurt that a single mother of four children raised me after leaving her abuser, and I mostly wore hand-me-downs. As a token of what seemed to be others' pity, people provided clothes, shoes, and other items for us to wear. With what my mother made from work, she would ensure that we had food and a roof over our heads, and for that, I am grateful. Nonetheless, a great majority of our money went to the church. My grandfather often took his whole check to the church. My mother did her best to care for us and did all she could to ensure we had everything we needed, but we lacked in the world's view of our reality. We lived in Milwaukee's inner city in neighborhoods where gunshots were the ambiance that rocked us to sleep on several occasions.

One particular evening, I remember being the most afraid as the police were raiding the house next door. An officer appeared at our duplex home, banging on our doors, telling us to get to the house's lowest place and stay there. Gunshots rang past our house as we sheltered in place, praying that we didn't get caught in the crossfire. That night the most disturbing thing happened to me. Awakened from my sleep, I could see everything around me, but I could not move or speak. Fear had gripped me, and there I lay, afraid, but could not scream or move.

After this experience, I was bound by fear, and I could tell no one.

I went to school day after day in fear of others hurting me and hurt by people who teased me, until the day that I had enough. I remember thinking, *I'm in sixth grade, and living in fear of my classmates must come to an end today.* It was the bully's unlucky day that he happened to be the one to provide the tease that was the final abuse that I could take, and I snapped. I yelled to him, "I have had enough!" It was then that he ran toward me, and in a panic I decided that instead of flight, I would fight. The feeling I felt as my fist collided with his face swiftly and consecutively was an experience of joy. It was as if years of pain released with every swing that landed on this class bully, and I felt free. I had finally released my bottled-up anxiety, but this joy was only for a moment, as the church found out about my suspension for fighting.

AUTHENTICITY INHIBITOR #11

If a man is to strike you, you turn the other cheek. It is a sin if you fight back and protect yourself; it doesn't matter if you look weak.

Preacher silenced me after being suspended for fighting. On Hopkins Street, Preacher would silence or not allow one to operate in the church if they broke the rules. I remember sitting in Preacher's office with my grandfather, having to explain why I defended myself from a guy who struck me first and had bullied me all year. They quoted the words of Matthew: "But I say unto you, That ye resist not evil: but whosoever shall smite thee on thy right cheek, turn to him the other also." (King James Version, Matthew 5:39). Another misinterpreted Scripture, where Preacher made it seem like protection of myself was somehow sinning. I didn't seek revenge, but I took a stance of defense in a moment where I felt threatened, and *Now I've embarrassed the family name again.*

I'm sure you can imagine what happened after embarrassing the family name again, in front of Preacher, once we got home. At this point, I no longer cared what they thought of me, but I wanted them to think I cared, so I took my lashing with stride and decided, *I'm going to do whatever I want to do; I'll ensure that they never know.* Algie's fury was now in full effect in my life, and I headed down the road of completely losing the man God intended me to be. I used that fury to mask the scared, hurt, insecure little boy who still lived on the inside. I was strong, smart, charismatic, and quick-witted to the world, but inside I was torn from my past experiences. No one could know how I felt, and no one could see my pain. I had mastered my disguise of being all put together on the outside but dead on the inside.

If you are reading this and identifying with any portion of this story that reminds you of you, remember you have a choice. I made choices in my life that were all wrong, and they led to me living in a world of false reality. Developing the characteristics of hypocrisy created a space where I could no longer identify myself. Darla's shame and Joyce's heartbreak were the final emotion to set with me before I finally embraced Darla's depression and, from there, David's hatred. The family emotions were yet together, and that is where I was taking a cliff dive, head first. However, it was also where I chose to break free, expose all within me, and start my unmasking journey.

CHAPTER 8

BRYAN'S REVIVAL

Bryan has several experiences that lead him into further despair until the life-changing encounter that leads him to revival after college.

Revivals were an integral part of my childhood. Preacher would call for multiple revivals throughout the year. Despite the revivals, with prayer and fasting to accompany, no one seemed to retain their victory from one revival to another. With so much church and so many evangelists, one might think that the whole church would be consumed with the power to obey God. The Hopkins Street Church was great at providing the people the emotional high they needed to forget about all their woes and to pour their pockets on the altar, but after that, they returned home to real issues.

I remember the first service that the preacher in the revival made me feel like I was with God. That service was the first time I had a Pentecostal experience; I was seven. That experience was like none other, and I will never forget that day. However, that day was just a day, because after I walked away to the next day, I didn't know enough about who God was to me not to drift astray slowly. As I continued to grow throughout life, struggling through school, I arrived at a place called puberty—a place where the girls' curves had caught my eyes and that feeling inside didn't subside, and remember, we don't talk about sex in the church. Until they tried. Yes, on Hopkins Street, they attempted to provide us with a consultation about dealing with our sexual desires. Their methodology was for us to take a cold shower.

It's the end of the eighth-grade year, I'm preparing for high school, and even if the showers were working, they were no longer working. After years of confinement and being sheltered from the world, my mother finally allowed me to go on a trip from home. Maybe to my benefit or maybe to my detriment, after the terrible things my mother endured, she was afraid of what would happen to us if she let us go. Now that I would be away, the freedom was beyond me, but I had a plan for this trip. I was not going to high school having my virginity intact, so I planned to do the deed on this trip. My mother often taught us not to be a fool, so against all the rules I packed preparation.

No one knew that I had failed in this way, and I later became afraid. Preacher taught that if a saint's kids didn't act according to the church's rules, their parents should put them out on the streets. Some complied with this rule, and now many of those children are adult casualties. I was afraid at that point that I'd be put out on the street, another loss because of my choice. So I then lived with yet another secret that no one knew, and I was convicted. Living with conviction is dangerous because it opens the door to living unruly when it's unresolved.

My unresolved conviction led to a secret life of sexual perversion coupled with a pornography addiction. That one act opened the door to immoral behaviors as I convinced myself that as long as I didn't lie with someone else, what I did with myself was allowed. I was struggling inside to keep it together; they all thought I was fine, but I was not. While Preacher exposed the wrongs of others around me publicly, I became surer than ever that I never wanted them to find out. I was so concerned with the image I portrayed that I hid my secret pains, hurting in silence.

Hopkins Street's culture was so toxic that no one ever truly got the support they needed to be authentic. Regardless of which "Zion" we marched in and out of as the church migrated from one building to another, from one freedom tree money scheme to a trip to Africa, which no one understood, the church's culture of hurt followed from Hopkins Street to every other place we landed. Many found themselves living behind a mask that hid their trauma until they exploded. I carried this culture with me throughout high school, making mistakes, pleasing my flesh, only to still feel the pain and bitterness that my father didn't love me enough to stay. I came to hate him. I was on the verge of an explosion.

Frequent emotional explosions became a recurring experience throughout the culture of the Hopkins Street Church. So I was right at home when I would bite someone's head off for doing something I didn't like. This type of behavior became the church's culture, masked as family love. The church accommodated broken people who learned to hide their pain in religious piety. This accommodation only lasted for those who toed the line, stroked the elite's ego, and ran in the circle of folks positioned with power. I was guilty by association because I, too, was living behind a mask that led me to sit in silence watching other hurt people hurt so many others.

This masked hurt culture became a way of life in the Hopkins Street Church, and we branded it as family. Unfortunately, this family was dysfunctional, and because of the isolation tactics that were a principle in this dysfunctional family, all we had was each other. Like an abusive relationship where one party flees only to return to that abuse again, my view of true love was perverted. From one relationship to another, I never knew how to truly be loved and allowed others to misuse and abuse me in search of their affection. Being naïve and gullible, I repeatedly found myself in heartbreaking positions.

Sheltered no more, I moved away for college, and for the first time, people received me for me; or so I thought. I had developed an alternate personality that was wild and dangerous, and I was part of the in-crowd, the marching band of the college. The truth was, no one came to football games to see the football team; they came to see the band. I was part of the sexy saxes, the group of saxophone players, and I think it's safe to say that I used that to my advantage. I had no problem fulfilling my flesh's desires on tour while embracing the Bible teacher's role on campus. I'd find time for hanging out while drinking and hotel parties, becoming what I dreaded, a hypocrite.

Completely torn due to the toxic environment I knew as a church, I had begun the practice of claiming to have moral standards to which my behaviors did not conform. One thing I did get from the Hopkins Church was an ability to recite the Word of God. I mean, I knew the Bible frontward and backward; it was in me. Everyone on campus knew me to be the guy who could teach about God. As I stood before a captive audience painting the picture of God, many converted, while I lived broken and, most of my days, in pain.

This pain continued until I met her. She caught my attention regardless of all the others who wanted my attention because she waited. She didn't throw herself at me, and for the first time, I felt like someone saw me. She had her quirky ways and different type of style for days, but she had my attention. Drawn to her aura, I felt like she was someone I needed to know. We met at first as she planned for me a birthday celebration. Honestly, I couldn't remember anyone ever doing that for me before, making me more interested in her. As time went on, we stayed connected, and in my mind, she was mine.

As time went by, we become closer, but we met one strange day, and she looked different. She came from a home not immersed in the church like mine, so she didn't know salvation as I was supposed to. However, she attended a church meeting down the road from campus, was baptized, and had a Pentecostal experience. She knew that I knew of this experience, as the first family of the church she attended came through Hopkins Street. She wondered why I never told her about this experience with God. I was running from the church while she was running toward it. I then had this feeling of conviction and condemnation repeatedly, and I didn't feel like I deserved her.

I fell into a place of depression, reliving my every action, and this would only be the beginning of this whirlwind of pain. My grades began to slip, and surviving college seemed more and more impossible, so I decided to give up. Right as I gave up, the phone rang, and it was my mom telling me that I needed to come home. Little did I know that this would be a trip home like no other because this is the last time, I would see my grandfather alive. His death hit me like a ton of bricks, as a light bulb went off in my head that he was the only "dad" I ever knew. Yes, other men were in my mother's life, but Grandpa seemingly had the answer to all things.

Despite his flaws, he was there for me in ways no other man had ever been, and there I was without a dad all over again. To me, David was a superhero, and it was unbearable to think that death had taken him away. That weekend was full of emotional explosions, from one family member to another, and all I wanted was to get out of that house. My mother and I even collided that weekend, so much so that my cousins and I stormed out of the house. The chaos surrounding his death was more than I could handle; immediately after his funeral, I returned to campus, more damaged than before.

After returning to campus, so much seemed different. It felt like I no longer fit in where I did before. People had moved on to other things, the band season had ended, and I felt alone. In this deep place of despair, I heard a voice say, "I am here; you were never alone. Come unto me, and I will give you everything you've been looking to obtain." It was then that I went to that church down the road from campus, and the opportunity to choose met me there. A choice is not something Preacher or anyone else at the Hopkins Street Church had ever offered me before.

Choices are essential in our ability to be authentic. In fact, since the beginning of time, God has given humanity choices. Teaching people that they have options that come with consequences helps them understand their role in intentionally choosing to be what God ordained them to be. God will be pleased in us making the right choice. The preacher that evening showed me God's authentic love, and God provided me with a choice—life more abundantly or death. Well, I had just experienced death, and frankly, my whole life seemed to have no life at all, so for the first time for me, I made the intentional choice to try real life in God.

This choice was mine, not from coercion or some spooky, mysterious scare tactic but from a place I had never felt before. After choosing to receive God in me, freeing myself from the pain of all the loss I had experienced, I understood the original purpose of my life. God was no longer just with me, but he was inside me, leading me and guiding me, teaching me how to overcome my grief. Finally, that void within me filled with the power of God's extraordinary abilities, the fuel that propelled me into my authentic destiny. Right there is where I got instructions from God to remove my mask.

You have journeyed with me through the pages of these stories to this place, and finally, the unmasking is here. Before proceeding, I caution you that the mask will come off only for those who have chosen to be freely authentic. The choice is yours to embrace all those hidden emotions and clinch them in your mind while deciding to choose life. If you have elected to choose life, I invite you to the unmasking. I invite you to take steps to reveal the true you and become all that God ordained you to be. Without further ado, ladies and gentlemen, let us proceed to unmask.

CHAPTER 9

REMOVING THE MASK

Learning to unmask with four simple steps called the MASK (**M**editation, **A**ffirmation, **S**alvation, and **K**nowledge)

Many make the mistake of believing that belief alone is enough. Faith is like fuel, a substance necessary for a motor to move, but until someone gets in the driver seat and executes the ignition producing combustion that starts the engine, the car full of fuel will never fulfill its purpose. Even after the motor begins, some action is necessary to cause movement of the object. James writes it in the spiritual like this: "Even so faith if it hath not works, is dead, being alone." (*King James Version*, James 2:17). To believe without action is to be full of faith or potential while never taking action with that faith to accomplish or produce one's purpose.

But simply believing that I could be free of the oppression of my past was not enough. I couldn't merely remove my mask without understanding the implications involved. Removing my facade would be matched with unfavorable opposition every step of the way. Paul writes it like this to the church of Rome: "I find then a law, that, when I would do good, evil is present with me" (*King James Version*, Romans 7:21). Throughout the journey of being unmasked, several events occurred, including returning home for good, and with the sense of humor of God, He required me to remove my mask right in the place where I put it on, the Hopkins Street Church.

Successful mask removal involves facing the trauma of your past. Often that means being unmasked will cause you to meet those traumas, reliving them as new traumas sometimes arise in the process. To survive this trauma, I developed a method that allowed me to use the M.A.S.K. to uncover my pain and authentically become all God wanted me to be. Unashamed, I demanded the respect that God commissioned me to obtain, living life freely. These principles occurred throughout my journey as the Hopkins Street Church took a turn for the worst.

> **M** | med·i·ta·tion /ˌmedəˈtāSH(ə)n/ – considering, pondering, computing, taking into account, calculating, speaking and communing to put into practice God's Word. "This book of the law shall not depart out of thy mouth, but thou shalt meditate therein day and night." (*King James Version*, Joshua 1:8)

Soon after my return, Preacher decided that he would sell the Hopkins Street Church, and into a wilderness we went. In this process, so many suffered as the ministry focused on raising enough money to get us to what he thought was the promised land. Confused in my mind as to what we were doing, I had to rely on the sweet communion of the Holy Ghost to comfort me as we went from one building to another, chasing a dream that seemed not to be God ordained.

Meditation clarifies God's plan for our lives as we communicate with Him in a secret place. It is the first action that activates one's faith. Remember that faith alone is dead, so meditation helps us plan what God wants out of our lives. It is during meditation that one becomes vulnerable to the will of God's pleasure. By breaking the hidden barriers in one's life, we break off the first portion of the masks that we wear. Meditating on the Word of God provides us with the opportunity to apply the principles of God to our lives properly.

We must do as Paul commanded for these principles to help us overcome the inevitable chaos around us. Paul writes to the Church of Phillipi, "Finally, brethren, whatsoever things are true, whatsoever things are honest, whatsoever things are just, whatsoever things are pure, whatsoever things are lovely, whatsoever things are of good report; if there be any virtue, and if there be any praise, think on these things" (*King James Version*, Philippians 4:8). Thinking and meditating on these things develops an ability for one to be confident in oneself. Meditation allows for one to see oneself the way God sees them and no longer in the light of self-hatred.

In the presence of God, I was able to find the richness of God's joy, receiving eternal pleasure. Even though I belonged to a church with no real home, I had fun in God. My focus was no longer pleasing Preacher; I was on a path to completely unmask. From this meditation came authentic worship that was directed directly at God. It didn't matter who else was in the room; when I would lead worship, it was me, and God and the words of my mouth became the meditation of my heart. No longer did I seek the acceptance of people; I only lived to please God.

Meditation is the first step to being unmasked. Unashamed and open before God, bring the totality of your problems before Him in exchange for rest. If you are at this stage, take a moment and plant your feet on the floor and open yourself to hearing the voice of God. Clear your mind of the chaos around you; it's just you and God. Say to him, *God, I want to be free. I choose to be open to You taking off the layers of this pain as You heal me deeply. I am here to commune with You, and I ask that You invite me into Your secret place.* In that secret place He invites you to, listen to His voice. The tears may flow, and the pain may hurt, but this is needful. It is the combustion you've needed to ignite your fuel of faith, and you're about to move.

Take this time with eyes still closed, full of tears and sweat, and embrace God. By this embrace, you must choose to forgive yourself for all the wrong you've committed and never let another soul make you feel condemned for what God has forgiven. As long as you keep moving forward, God will never leave you. He is with you and is your present help despite what trouble comes your way. After this embrace, you are ready to hear God. Ask Him for guidance and direction, and He will speak in a small, still voice, and you will know it is He. This process is not a race, and it's not about the strongest. Don't move from this place in your heart until you hear from Him. The next step to being unmasked will not apply until you have listened to and can identify his voice.

> **A** | af·firm·a·tion /ˌafərˈmāSH(ə)n/ – stating, declaring, asserting, making sure of through confirmation, that something is factual with confidence. "I have given my word and affirmed it to keep your righteous judgments." (*International Standard Version*, 1995/2014, Psalm 119:106)

A driver who has just started the car would be reckless to begin moving without confirming that everything around them is safe. Failure to establish confirmation of safety could result in a dangerous collision that could be fatal for all who are onboard the vehicle and the lives of others involved outside. Additionally, merely moving with no clear and confirmed direction can lead to a waste of fuel and time, two precious resources needed to get wherever one desires to be. Remember, faith is our fuel in this process, and we don't want to waste it.

To ensure proper fuel of faith preservation, one must affirm what they heard in the meditation phase of being unmasked. Even if those around you are moving swiftly out of pride and emotion, you stand still until you've affirmed the voice of God. Unfortunately, the Hopkins Street Church carried me and others from place to place, all the way to a place called God's City. However, it seemed that He didn't reside in what we called His city, and there more people became casualties of a word heard in meditation that seemed to lack real affirmation.

The affirming process can be elusive, and sometimes it seems that it will never come, but you wait. You sit there and meditate until you affirm that God has told you to move so that others don't become victims of your haste to have something that God may not have ordained you to have. You wait until God gives you His word and affirms it. You'll know it's affirmation because He'll begin providing the tools needed for the journey. Check your surroundings and pack everything He tells you to before your move. Unfortunately, failure to confirm the Hopkins Street Church's rapid movement left tons of people in the wind, grasping for help with their pain and toil. Regrettably, many like me stayed, migrating from building to building, being drained with no reprieve, all to keep the church together for the sake of Preacher.

When we fail to affirm God's plan for our life, we may move prematurely, taking on more than we have the grace to handle in that time. It will be beautiful and alluring, and many will praise you for what you have, but while you're on the move, you're running over people with no regard, and this is dangerous. Especially when God has entrusted you with the souls of men and placed them in your care, you can't take the chance with their lives. Their lives are not yours to gamble. We must wait patiently, testing out every spirit that speaks to us, affirming that they are of God.

Affirmation is the second step toward being unmasked. Remember, God does not lie nor repent. If he says something, he intends to see it through. If you are at this stage, take a moment and take inventory of everything around you and everything you have. Identify what has connected to you that might hinder you from moving when God says move. Begin making a plan for the successful execution of God's will in your life. Say to Him, *God, I want to know Your voice and keep Your commandments. I want to be all You want me to be; show me Thy path and make it straight.* As the way becomes more evident, the second part of the mask will begin to fall off.

Now with your eyes closed, return to that secret place where God has invited you before and begin speaking to Him what you heard Him say. You will start to feel His presence, and if God agrees with the plan that you developed, you will feel alignment with His affirmation. Believe that He will, in his time, give you the assurance you need to proceed. Embrace those things that He instructs you to move out of your way so that you don't hurt others as you progress. Adjust your sights from feelings within to thoughts of those around as you prepare for His clearance to move. Be still until He affirms your next move, for failure to do so could make you miss out on the next step to being unmasked.

> S | sal·va·tion /salˈvāSH(ə)n/ – preserving, conserving, reclaiming, delivering, and redeeming from harm, ruin, or loss. "And you also were included in Christ when you heard the message of truth, the gospel of your salvation. When you believed, you were marked in him with a seal, the promised Holy Spirit." (*New International Version*, 1973/2011, Ephesians 1:13)

Once the driver pulls out and begins the journey, it becomes essential that the driver acknowledge safety. They must follow the signs posted on the road, traveling safely. It is best when one has a clear plan for how they will arrive at their destination. Failing to do so could result in missing travel directions, ending up at the wrong goal temporarily, or worst, never coming to any destination at all. Failure to comply with the road rules could lead one to a citation, sanctions, and even imprisonment.

I found myself living in a place of imprisonment as the Hopkins Street Church was dwindling to nothing at all. I felt that I had invested so much into this that seeing it fade away was hard, but I had to receive the salvation God was providing from the chaos of that church. Beware that you don't miss your exit being concerned with things you've attached to yourself. That was me, trying to save a thing that God wanted finished. I even found myself neglecting myself, from courtrooms to business meetings, trying to save what was not mine to hold, while God was trying to keep me. God freed me from the prison that I lived in for most of my life, posed as a church.

Once I released it all into the hands of God, I truly became free. It was at that moment I received true salvation from all that I harbored inside. After making room in my heart, I made room for more, and then I genuinely had space for someone else to love. After embracing salvation and allowing God to free me, I chose to let someone else in to love. It must have been God led because she whom I referred to from college waited for me. Through ups and downs, break-ups, and missteps while dating, Geraldineia became my wife. She is now my helpmeet and confidant.

Embracing salvation means letting go of the past, setting your desire on the things of Christ. This freedom will allow you to receive the blessings of the Lord. When you hear from the Lord and affirm His will for you through the message of the gospel, salvation will be yours. Salvation sealed with the promises of God comes with the sure guarantee of the Holy Spirit. Christ promised to send us a Comforter in time of need, and that Comforter is the Holy Spirit. He will lead and guide us into the truth of who God desires us to be.

Salvation is the third step in the unmasking process. The Holy Spirit became my guide like never before, showing me the error of others' ways and the erroneous pattern I committed myself. The Holy Spirit should be the plan that ensures you arrive at God's authentic place for your life. He should direct you to sound guidance and leadership, providing you with counsel on whom you connect to while leading you in all aspects of your life. The Holy Spirit allows for intentional and deliberate actions that are God led. Salvation comes through belief in God but requires effort to be complete. After deliverance, the third part of the mask will fall.

Now with your eyes locked toward heaven, accept Christ as your Lord and Savior. Accept His spirit within you, leaning not to your thoughts but His will in your life. Receive His plan of salvation, which includes the cleansing of one's sins by way of immersion in water through baptism and wait for Him to fill you with His Holy Spirit as He promised in His Word. Ask Christ to change your mind, providing you with a newness that only knows the love of God. Wait for salvation, for it is essential to getting out of the place of despair we've found ourselves. With redemption obtained, we now are prepared for the final step to being unmasked.

> **K** | knowl·edge /ˈnäləj/ – knowing, understanding, realizing, and accurately comprehending God's Word. "My people are destroyed for lack of knowledge." (*King James Version*, Hosea 4:6)

Frequent maintenance of a vehicle is essential to the longevity of the car's life. When one understands when to change their oil or refuel, it makes them better equipped to maintain the vehicle. These are two crucial knowledge points for any car owner to know. There are times when one will run into a problem with their vehicle and have no knowledge of how to diagnose it or even fix it. In these cases, it is vital to have a trusted advisor who is knowledgeable and tactful in helping you address your car's concerns. This professional should demonstrate competency in auto mechanics. They should know the subject and possess the wisdom to apply that knowledge appropriately, based on the situation. They must also have the emotional stability to interact with you, providing comfort and trust in them as individuals.

After the Hopkins Street Church dissolved, we were left with little knowledge and absent a trusted advisor who could address the frequent maintenance essential to our salvation's longevity. It forced me to dig into my first love of learning and search the Scriptures for myself. Having an advisor who is competent and wise is essential. However, it is just as vital that you know enough for yourself not to allow misleading. We ought to study for ourselves, learning how to apply God's plan to our lives specifically. We should be unashamed to come boldly to God and seek His wisdom.

When we leave it to someone else to make decisions for us, we deny God's power through salvation. Without knowledge and the wisdom to properly apply knowledge, others' demands to act, talk, walk, and live a certain way become our life's reality. God has allowed us to learn of Him, and no one knows us better than He does. He is gentle and humble in heart, and He wants to uplift us to places beyond what we can ask or think. We must seek knowledge for ourselves, saving ourselves from this world. Had I not embraced the experience that I had, I would have made choices that could have led me back into bondage.

So many have made fatal mistakes because they did not know. Some have rejected knowledge; therefore, God has rejected them. Others have allowed those around them, and even those in leadership, to solely think for them. Because they have forgotten the laws of God, God has forgotten them. We must remember that God is jealous and wants no other gods before Him, including other people. Yes, we ought to respect those in authority who lead us but not to the extent that God's worship points to any person. Be sure that your trusted advisor is indeed tactful, using wisdom to apply their knowledge while demonstrating emotional health themselves.

Knowledge is the fourth and final step in the unmasking process. The time has come for the last piece of your mask to fall, and understanding is the power to keep the disguise off. With knowledge, others cannot hoax you into the belief of unsupported church legislation, which hinders you from being who God truly ordained you to be. Wisdom rejects the imposition of authenticity inhibitors that breed the brokenness you once had. Being knowledgeable allows one to choose the path of their life according to the salvation they received, aligning their decisions to a personal understanding of God's Word.

Now with your eyes opened, be vigilant and sober-minded, always aware of your surroundings. Pray before you read God's Word and ask him to open your understanding and your mind to the knowledge He would want to impart into you. Embrace a trusted advisor, such as a pastor or spiritual father, to guide you on applying the Word of God in your life. When you study, don't be ashamed to seek an understanding and ask why. Why allows for more in-depth development of the knowledge God wants us to receive. It is okay to ask why. Don't let anyone place you in a box of only retrieving knowledge through them; that is not God ordained. Embrace the experience of hearing God for yourself. After receiving proper knowledge, you have officially unmasked, having chosen to be free, knowing that you are on a path intentionally designed for you by God.

Now that you are unmasked, don't make the mistake of believing that replacing your mask is not possible. Without adequately addressing your feelings and pain routinely, all the work you just accomplished could be all for naught if the disguise begins to mend together and ends up back on your face. Meditation is a continuous process that we perform day and night. Affirmation should be part of our routine to ensure we are always on the course God intended for us. Salvation comes by faith, and without faith, it impossible to please God or yourself. Finally, knowledge is indeed power and must be consistently updated to remain relevant in any dispensation of God's grace.

God's grace is sufficient for us to stay mask-free. He desires that we live life authentically, free from our families' generational curses and the pain inflicted by others who couldn't dissect the pain they had themselves. We must be brave and confident in the face of opposition, relying on God to be our defense. Understand that not everyone will be happy that you have unmasked. Satan and those who choose to be used by him will seek to ensure your mask never comes off or that it returns inevitably. Therefore, we must know Satan's tactics and prepare ourselves for life mask-free, which I call the "after-mask."

CHAPTER 10

THE AFTER-MASK

Learning to live authentically after unmasking, being all that God ordained us to be, freely.

Let me be the first to congratulate you for taking this journey. With God's help, you have made it to the after-mask. The after-mask is the state of being that occurs once one has become free from past trauma. Becoming unmasked was the easy part; now, we have to do the work to remain in liberty. Many will view your new authenticity as a threat to their ability to remain a silent perpetrator of authenticity inhibitors. Others will find jealousy in their hearts as you flourish, reaping the results of God's blessing plan for those who live authentically. There will even be those with more power than you, who have masked insecurities and will find ways to attempt suppression of your abilities, to box you back into a place of unauthentic life. The after-mask begins when we choose that the life we live now will not be governed by them but by grace.

We now have the power to show grace because, in the after-mask, we are G.R.A.C.E. The after-mask allows us to:

- **G**ive unselfishly;

- **R**ejoice unashamedly;
- **A**dvocate unbiasedly;
- **C**ommunicate unfearfully; and
- **E**mpower unreluctantly.

However, we must seal this G.R.A.C.E. with forgiveness. We must start with forgiving ourselves for the part we played in our mask. In the after-mask, we will finally realize that some of our choices were self-gratifying; they were our fault. The truth is, while others may have influenced our life's intentions, and in some cases, we were fearful or uninformed, they never had the power to choose for us unless we gave that power to them. Whether those choices were good or bad, they were ours to make, and in the after-mask, we have finally realized that we are in charge of our destiny and choices.

I made choices even in telling this story because in the after-mask we understand that some things are better left unsaid; it's called temperance. Certain things go unmentioned in this story, even though they, too, brought much trauma. Several turns of events that took place in the Hopkins Street Church caused damage that still resides in the lives of many, but I choose not to give those things power. I do this purposely, as I subscribe to what I prescribe to be the spotlight principle. This principle is the phenomenon that occurs in times where we take something which God has made insignificant and make it significant merely by giving it a spot in the light. Some things don't deserve the spotlight; doing so allows them to be more prevalent in our lives than God expects. Additionally, if one's toxic behaviors receive a platform, they are now on a stage for all to see, sometimes unnecessarily making others a casualty of their performances.

When we operate in G.R.A.C.E., we learn to let some performances go unnoticed—leave them in the dark. We ought to leave some things in the dark, not by masking them, but rather keeping them in plain sight and praying for them. Our forgiveness toward those who showed us no remorse is the most unselfish act of grace we can provide. The Word of God says, "But I say unto you, love your enemies, bless them that curse you, do good to them that hate you, and pray for them which despitefully use you, and persecute you" (*King James Version*, Matthew 5:44). Living in the after-mask makes this possible. Our prayer for them is that God would lead them into an encounter where they, too, can be unmasked. In the after-mask, we hope that they will obtain abundance, because we have everything we need in the after-mask.

We have all that we need because we've learned, in the after-mask, to *give unselfishly*. In the after-mask, you understand the value of allowing the principles of giving to be part of our lives, not just our monetary gifts but we must contribute from all our abilities. In the after-mask, we learn to support the weak and remember the words of Jesus saying, "It is more blessed to give than to receive." When I was in pain, I could not see past myself. I failed to realize the value of doing for others. Service to God and His people with no selfish agenda is a characteristic I obtained in the after-mask. One shouldn't ignore their own needs, but instead we should put in perspective that our gifts are not just for ourselves but all. Giving selflessly allows God to continuously provide blessings that overflow consistently in the lives of those in the after-mask.

As we live in the after-mask, we learn to *rejoice unashamedly* about what God has done in our lives. Those who still hide behind a mask may be uncomfortable, as their jealousy will not allow them to receive unashamed praise in every aspect of our life. Even though we are commanded in God's Word to bless the Lord at all times, there will be those who will wish you would be silent about God's favor in your life. In the after-mask, our worship is authentic, unconstrained by our current circumstances or any other person's thought of it. Our praise and our worship belong to God. Rejoicing without shame allows God to trust us with blessings more abundantly as we live in the after-mask.

Living in the after-mask creates a yearning for one to *advocate unbiasedly* for ourselves and those we encounter. Some will dislike us for interfering with their plans to destroy, but we support right without prejudice, partiality, or partisanship in the after-mask. In today's contentious political climate, even those who claim to be the called of God have found themselves compromising what's right to fit within their traditions of partiality and their prejudiced teachings that don't align with God's Word. This story is my advocacy, absent any bias, just merely revealing the pain that I and others have faced in hopes that we might make a change for what is right. Advocating without nepotism or preconception allows for God's righteous judgment to be upheld in the lives of all who live in the after-mask.

In the lives of those who live in the after-mask, we *communicate* the Word of God *unfearfully*. With boldness, we profess the will of God through the gospel of Jesus Christ. Effective communication does well for all parties involved and ensures that we identify our actions' objectives with clarity. Often fear grips one to the point of having an inability to speak when God tells us to. I lived in this space before removing my mask, but now in the after-mask, I am unashamed and unafraid to speak under the authority of Jesus Christ. In the after-mask, elevation in ministry and spiritual development came freely. Preaching the Word of God became a power unto salvation. I believed that the words of my mouth were indeed the meditations of my heart. God promises this life to all. Communicating without fear allows God to use freely all who believe and live in the after-mask.

The after-mask provides for those who live within to *empower unreluctantly* ourselves and those around us. We have the opportunity in the after-mask to have all things in life and godliness. The world belongs to us because God has given it to those who live in the after-mask. In the after-mask, I realized that I had the power to command things to be in my life by the words of my mouth. Therefore, I began speaking those things that I wanted to see, even before seeing them as I watched them come to the past. I received both a bachelor's degree in the after-mask, which I failed to receive before and even a master's degree, which my past didn't anticipate. These degrees weren't merely for me, but they are instead for the knowledge to empower those around me. Empowering others with no hesitation allows for freedom to ring in the lives of all who live in the after-mask.

G.R.A.C.E. lives in the after-mask and allows us to choose to remain free. We must reject others' claim to fame by not giving them influence over our lives, providing grace to combat their will to perpetuate their pain onto us. The reality is that those that are guilty of inflicting pain on others are, in most cases, hurt themselves, so we ought to pray for them. Remember that we must seal G.RA.C.E. through forgiveness. If one is to live in the after-mask successfully, we must choose grace and forgiveness. No, I don't subscribe to the thought that you must forget, but you absolutely must let go of their hold on your life through forgiveness. They require the same grace that God afforded to us, and that grace begins with us.

Through this journey, we have come so far from pain to purpose after being unmasked. You now live in the after-mask and must make a choice every day to remain free. You must stand confident in your freedom, always trusting in the plan of God in your life. Many may provide opinions on how you ought to live, and some of it will be wise counsel that we should receive. However, always remember to align their counsel with the Word of God and G.R.A.C.E. The after-mask is yours to have forever as long as you hold on to it. The Lord of peace himself will give you peace always. The Lord is with us in the after-mask.

CONCLUSION

The year is now 2021, and still, everyone is wearing a physical mask. While this physical mask remains, many of us have now unmasked the emotional pain that we contained, giving it to God, who has allowed us to live in the after-mask. We are no longer ashamed of who we are and have decided to demand that we received the liberty and peace God promised to our fathers if we trusted in Him. We are now not only doing our part to remain free from a virus that still plagues society, but we are also fighting to stay free of the oppression built by unsupported church legislation that hindered us from living authentically. We fight to hold on to the peace we received after finally breathing the breath of life, freely, once we unmasked.

I am no longer afraid of the painful intentions of those whose actions tried to destroy me, because with my mask off, I can see them. I no longer hide hateful feelings of disgust, because I live in a place where I trust that God can and will fight these battles on my behalf. Despite the racial injustice that I have experienced at the police's hands, who now boldly display their hatred for my skin color, I choose to be unafraid and live life authentically. I am comfortable with expressing my true inner self because it is pure. My struggle internally with my emotions is an everyday battle, but it no longer hinders me from being my authentic self.

To the fury of Algie, I say, *Goodbye! No longer will you make me lash out in haste, but instead, I will be patient and slow to wrath.* To the hatred of David, I say, *So long! I will love myself and others as this is the commandment of God.* To the heartbreak of Joyce, *I dismiss you. I will forgive those who mistreated me and despitefully used me; this is God's will for my life.* To Darla's insecurity, shame, and depression, *You must go!* I have too much power in me, and God has been too faithful toward me, so I will not dwell in the pains of yesterday, today, or tomorrow. These seeds I cancel in my life. This generational curse ends with me.

I speak to myself that no one has the power to inhibit me from being authentic. I will experience real purpose. I will be the man that my wife and children deserve, giving them all of me indefinitely. I will not struggle with inferiority thoughts, but I will speak that God says I am all that my family needs with Him. I will be free to uniquely be the man of knowledge God made me, boldly and without reserve. I will not allow the intimidation of others to box me into believing that being open, bold, and courageous somehow make me abrasive; I will use God's abilities as he has provided them to me. I am who I AM says I am.

This family curse is not who God says I am; it is not mine to hold. I release my pain of fatherlessness into the hand of the God who allowed it. I won't bottle up my emotions and fall victim to the mysterious nature of traditional ways unfounded by God's plan for man, perpetuating society's ideological force, where my children know not God in the fullness of His power. I will not stifle my children's inquisitive nature for knowledge and be confident enough in who I am to allow them to be all God wants them to be, even if that surpasses me. I will not breed trauma around them, and should they experience trauma within or without my control, I will have enough wisdom to take them to God and a counselor.

My children will know the call of God on their lives. I will teach them that Daddy's words must align with God's Word, and when they don't, they are my opinion alone. My children will develop minds of their own, and my only prayer is that I have trained them up so that when they create those minds, they don't depart from God. I will encourage them to be open and honest and not hide their feelings. I will teach them healthy temperance, addressing their emotions, seeking help when necessary. Even if it means I must decrease that they might increase, I will be humble enough to allow God to elevate them where He desires.

Only those who have unmasked can boldly proclaim these words. Those who live in meditation and affirm that God's salvation and knowledge are with them can be all God expects them to be for themselves and their families. I will give unselfishly, rejoice unashamedly, advocate unbiasedly, communicate unfearfully, and empower unreluctantly. I have identified my true identity and embraced genuine authenticity. I have overcome the family curse, and I'm making strides to become all God created me to be. I intend to reap the benefit of the new seeds I have planted in myself and my family. You, too, can uproot those old seeds and toss out those generational curses and experience with me authentic purpose, unmasked.

www.ingramcontent.com/pod-product-compliance
Lightning Source LLC
LaVergne TN
LVHW010921110826
845155LV00038B/688

* 9 7 8 1 9 5 2 3 2 7 4 9 0 *